T0015659

APPALOOSA HORSES

by Alissa Thielges

AMICUS

pattern

hoof

Look for these words and pictures as you read.

mane

foal

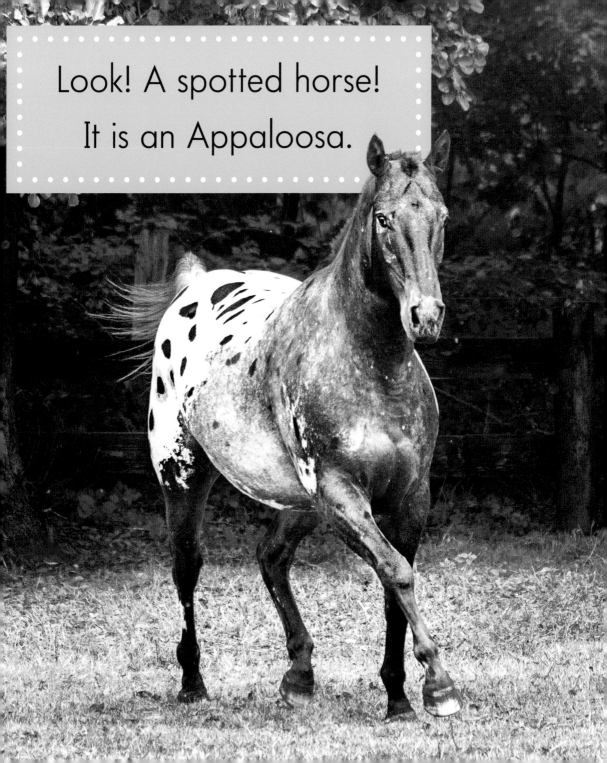

Look! A spotted horse!

It is an Appaloosa.

See the pattern?
It is called leopard.
There are a lot of spots.

pattern

See the hoof?
It is hard.
It has stripes.

hoof

mane

See the mane?
It is short and thin.
The tail is short, too.

An Appaloosa is smart.

It turns quickly.

It wins events.

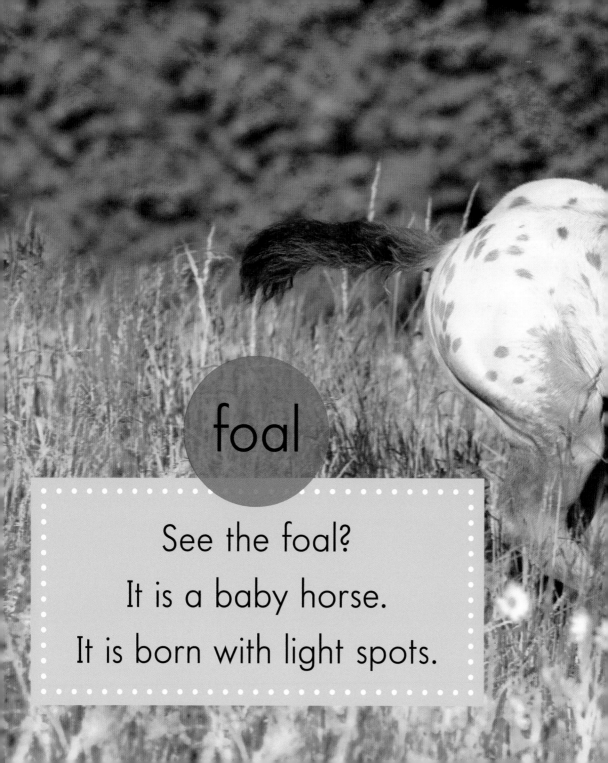

foal

See the foal?

It is a baby horse.

It is born with light spots.

The foal grows up.
Its spots get darker.

See the pattern?
It is called leopard.
There are a lot of spots.

pattern

See the hoof?
It is hard.
It has stripes.

hoof

pattern

hoof

Did you find?

mane

foal

mane

See the mane?
It is short and thin.
The tail is short, too.

foal

See the foal?
It is a baby horse.
It is born with light spots.

Spot is published by Amicus
P.O. Box 227, Mankato, MN 56002
www.amicuspublishing.us

Library of Congress Cataloging-in-Publication Data
Names: Thielges, Alissa, 1995- author.
Title: Appaloosa horses / by Alissa Thielges.
Description: Mankato, Minnesota : Amicus, [2023] | Series: Spot horses | Audience: Ages 4–7 | Audience: Grades K–1 | Summary: "Meet the Appaloosa horse breed in this leveled reader that reinforces key vocabulary with a search-and-find feature that builds new vocabulary and creates a successful foundation for emergent readers."– Provided by publisher.
Identifiers: LCCN 2021055471 (print) | LCCN 2021055472 (ebook) | ISBN 9781645492443 (hardcover) | ISBN 9781681527680 (paperback) | ISBN 9781645493327 (ebook)
Subjects: LCSH: Appaloosa horse--Juvenile literature.
Classification: LCC SF293.A7 T45 2023 (print) | LCC SF293.A7 (ebook) | DDC 636.1/3--dc23/eng/20211213
LC record available at https://lccn.loc.gov/2021055471
LC ebook record available at https://lccn.loc.gov/2021055472

Rebecca Glaser, editor
Deb Miner, series designer
Catherine Berthiaume and Grant Gould, book design and photo research

Photos by Shutterstock/Picsoftheday cover, Julia Remezova 1, mveldhuizen 3, Lenkadan 4–5, Makarova Viktoria 6–7, Zuzule 8–9, Lenkadan 12–13; Dreamstime/Tommcginty 10–11; Alamy/Mark J. Barrett 14–15

APPALOOSA HORSES